Original title:
Celestial Chuckles

Copyright © 2025 Creative Arts Management OÜ
All rights reserved.

Author: Ryan Sterling
ISBN HARDBACK: 978-1-80567-819-9
ISBN PAPERBACK: 978-1-80567-940-0

Dancing on Cosmic Clouds

Up above, the stars do sway,
With fluffy clouds that twist and play.
A cosmic jig, a merry sight,
As planets twirl in joyful flight.

With comets playing tag so bright,
Galaxies giggle, pure delight.
Asteroids laugh and tumble too,
In this vast sky, joy feels so new.

Mischievous Moonlit Memoirs

The moon winks down with silver beams,
Painting the night with silly dreams.
A frog in tux, in puddles hops,
While starlit shorts reveal no stops.

The shadows dance with giddy grace,
A cat in a top hat wins the race.
With swirling whispers, stories brew,
As laughter sparkles in the dew.

Starlight Silliness

Oh, twinkling lights that giggle high,
They tickle clouds that drift on by.
A playful wink from Venus' eye,
As laughter echoes in the sky.

Jupiter jests, the big clown there,
While Saturn spins with rings to share.
They pull a prank, a cosmic tease,
A funny dance among the trees.

Lunar Laughs and Jests

Oh, the moon beams down a cheeky grin,
While crickets chirp their secret spin.
A rocket's roar, a catapult,
As stardust plays the jester's cult.

With every wink, the craters sing,
The night unfolds a joyous fling.
In the darkness, giggles rise,
As pals tickle the velvet skies.

Starlit Serenades of Fun

Under the moon, the stars do wink,
Comets dance, don't you think?
Galaxies giggle, oh what a sight,
Meteor showers bring pure delight.

Planets play tag in the night sky,
Black holes burp as they float by.
In this cosmic playground so bright,
The universe chuckles with all its might.

The Jovial Dance of Infinity

Spinning around in a joyful spree,
Saturn's rings jingle, can you see?
With each twirl, there's laughter to share,
The cosmos grins, floating on air.

Nebulas puff and puff with glee,
Supernovae pop, oh what a spree!
The fabric of space in stitches it bends,
As the laughter of worlds never ends.

Starlit Laughter

Twinkling lights make merry sounds,
Eclipses play peek-a-boo all around.
With each twinkle, giggles abound,
In the vast sky, joy can be found.

Constellations wink with a sly game,
Starry jests, never the same.
The cosmos thrives in its playful art,
With each chuckle, it steals our heart.

Cosmic Giggles

In the vastness, a chuckle is heard,
Asteroids zoom like a playful bird.
Shooting stars flash with a grin so wide,
Come join the fun, take a ride!

A galaxy spins in a giggling whirl,
In spacetime's fabric, the laughter unfurls.
With every glance at the cosmic view,
There's magic and mirth, just for you.

Playful Pulsars

In the dance of stars, they twirl and spin,
With a wink and a giggle, they let joy in.
Radios crackle, laughter in their beams,
Winking at the cosmos, fulfilling our dreams.

Tickling the void with their joyful strife,
Pulsating rhythms of interstellar life.
They play peek-a-boo with meteors so bright,
Inviting the galaxies to join their delight.

Cosmic Chuckle Anew

A comet whizzes by with a cheeky grin,
Sprinkling stardust wherever it's been.
Planets giggle as they spin in line,
Creating a symphony of cosmic design.

Nebulae swirl in a dance of glee,
Painting the sky with colors so free.
While black holes chuckle, oh, what a sight,
Sucking in laughter and dousing the night.

Charmed by the Cosmos

The Milky Way whispers jokes in the night,
While meteors giggle in their fiery flight.
Stars beam brightly, their laughter a song,
Creating a harmony where all things belong.

A galaxy spins with a playful tease,
Poking at moons like a gentle breeze.
Cosmic wonders filled with cheer and fun,
As laughter erupts from each distant sun.

The Laughter of the Universe

The cosmos chuckles in a vibrant hue,
As planets do pirouettes, just for you.
Asteroids caper in a quirky dance,
Inviting us all to take a chance.

The constellations smirk with delight,
Winking at Earth as we watch the night.
With every flicker and sparkling light,
The universe giggles, what a joyful sight!

Interstellar Smirks

In the void, stars wink bright,
Planets spin with sheer delight.
Asteroids dance in cheeky flair,
While comets zoom without a care.

Galaxies swirl with cosmic jest,
Laughter echoes, a starry fest.
Supernovas pop with a cheer,
In the galaxy's wild joke frontier.

A quasar's beam, a jesting ray,
Protons giggle as they play.
Black holes chuckle at the fun,
Swirling wild 'til day is done.

Cosmic Giggles in Orbit

There's a moon that loves to tease,
Tickling asteroids with the breeze.
Saturn's rings spin round and round,
Making laughter's silly sound.

Mars threw a party, all aglow,
With Martian friends in line to show.
Venus twirled in golden flight,
Making sure the night's just right.

Stars exchange jokes, a stellar crowd,
While meteors streak, oh so loud.
In this vast, amusing dance,
Every comet takes a chance.

Celestial Comedy Hour

The sun cracks jokes about the day,
While clouds giggle, drifting away.
Rain drops laughing in the sun's warm light,
Creating puddles of pure delight.

Neptune tells tales with a sly grin,
While friends all chuckle, letting fun in.
Uranus joins with a joke so grand,
Spinning laughter across the land.

Jupiter joins, the largest one,
Says, "Let's keep this laughter fun!"
Stars burst into giggles bright,
Making night a laugh-filled sight.

The Playful Planetarium

A planetarium full of glee,
Shows shooting stars in harmony.
Kids laugh out loud, reaching high,
As planets bounce and twirl nearby.

The rings of Saturn joke and sway,
While a meteor giggles all the way.
Pulsars blink with a cheeky beat,
To the rhythm of this cosmic treat.

Celestial bodies break into song,
Cosmic humor where all belong.
In this whimsical night's embrace,
Laughter twinkles through the space.

The Lighthearted Cosmos

Stars winks like they know a joke,
The moon giggles, it's no hoax.
Planets spin in a merry dance,
While comets wink in a playful prance.

Asteroids laugh with a little flair,
Whispering secrets in the moonlit air.
Space dust tickles the cosmic nose,
As laughter bubbles, the universe glows.

Comedic Constellations

Orion trips over his shining belt,
While Cassiopeia just laughs and knelt.
Ursa Major chuckles at the sight,
Of tiny stars in a dizzy flight.

Shooting stars make a wish that's bold,
But probably end up just being told,
That in this expanse, humor's the key,
And laughter echoes from sea to sea.

Giggling through the Galaxy

Planets play tag through the darkened skies,
While Jupiter shares silly, starlit lies.
Saturn laughs with its rings in a swirl,
As cosmic pranks make the stardust twirl.

Nebulae bloom with colors so bright,
As starlings chuckle in pure delight.
Galaxies spin in a comical way,
Creating giggles through night and day.

Playful Planets

Mercury zips with a cheeky grin,
While Venus sways, letting the fun begin.
Mars tosses jokes with a gentle flair,
And laughter shoots through Martian air.

Neptune laughs, splashing waves of mirth,
While Saturn spins tales of great worth.
In this cosmic game, there's joy to share,
With every twinkle, we float without care.

Lively Little Asteroids

In a dance through the night,
Little rocks spin with delight.
They tumble and bounce, oh what a sight,
Each one giggles, feeling just right.

Their paths may cross, but they won't collide,
With a wink and a twirl, they glide.
Whispering jokes as they take a ride,
On this wild cosmic joyride.

Heaven's Hilarious Highlights

Stars wink like they're in on a joke,
Puffs of space laugh at every poke.
Planets spin tales, with comets to cloak,
Together they form a stellar smoke.

Meteor showers burst with surprise,
Gifting us laughter from the skies.
Celestial gaffes, no need for goodbyes,
In this joyful realm where humor lies.

Stellar Smiles and Snickers

A sunbeam tickles the darkened sky,
While moons chuckle, their glow is spry.
Galaxies swirl with a wink and a sigh,
In this endless giggle, we easily fly.

Every twinkle shares a secret glee,
Eclipses pull pranks, oh can't you see?
In this expanse of cosmic esprit,
Laughter echoes through infinity.

Cosmic Chuckle Festival

Gather round, stars are in a spree,
Planets party, what a jubilee!
Comets race, trying to agree,
On the best punchlines from A to Z.

Witty quips from the nebula crew,
Asteroids snort, it's quite the view.
In this festival where gags ensue,
Laughter reigns, the night feels anew.

Nebula's Nefarious Nods

In the corner of the sky, a giggle swirls,
Stars play peek-a-boo, as laughter unfurls.
Planets bounce and jiggle in galactic glee,
While comets take selfies, wild and free.

Asteroids throw parties, so wild and bright,
Meteor showers dance, a dazzling sight.
With every twinkle, a joke takes flight,
The universe chuckles, deep into the night.

Dancing with Celestial Bodies

Twinkling partners spin in cosmic delight,
While moons crack jokes, causing stars to ignite.
Pulsars and quasars join in a waltz,
Even black holes grin, defying all faults.

Galaxies gossip in the great big space,
Trading puns that make comets race.
With every twist, the void fills with cheer,
Laughter echoes, filling the atmosphere.

The Humor of the Heavens

In the vacuum of space, a punchline is born,
Where gravity tickles, and dark matter's worn.
Supernovae giggle, bursting forth with flair,
While aliens chuckle at the sight of their hair.

Shoot for the stars, they say with a grin,
As cosmic ventriloquists make planets spin.
Their humor is vast, as vast as the sky,
A joyful riddle no one can deny.

Laughter Among the Stars

Stars whisper secrets, with twinkling smiles,
While Venus and Mars share hilarious wiles.
Each night they gather for a cosmic roast,
As meteorites share stories they love the most.

Neptune cracks jokes that even light can't catch,
While Jupiter's band plays a catchy match.
With each orbit, laughter fills the night air,
A chorus of giggles, swirling with flair.

Vortexes of Joy

In a swirling dance, stars twirl with glee,
Giggles echo through the night sky free.
Asteroids wearing hats, quite the sight,
Shooting stars wink with a playful light.

Planets play tag in a cosmic race,
Jupiter's grin is a jovial face.
While comets toss confetti on passersby,
Each laugh a ripple in the darkened sky.

Whimsical Wonders of the Heavens

A moonbeam's tickle makes craters giggle,
Clouds shape animals in a spacey wiggle.
Meteor showers clapping with delight,
While aliens chuckle, oh what a night!

Galaxies spin with their own funny flair,
Supernovae burst with a cosmic scare.
Twinkling stars play peek-a-boo games,
In this sky full of joy, no one's to blame.

Quirks of the Quasars

Quasars chuckle, bright as a sun,
Whirling and twirling, oh what fun!
They flash silly faces, hide and seek,
Cosmic jesters, unique and bleak.

Nebulas puff in hues so bright,
Creating shapes that spark pure delight.
In the breach of night, with a wink and a spar,
The universe laughs from near and far.

Laughter Across Light Years

Across the cosmos, laughter does fly,
Echoing softly, in the night sky.
Stars toast with tangy space drinks,
While waving to planets with winks and blinks.

Galactic giggles spark like fire,
Building a fun that you can admire.
Every light year a new joke unfolds,
In the vastness, humor never grows old.

Twilight Tickle

In the fading light, stars start to grin,
Winking at shadows, come join the spin.
Moonbeams are giggling, wearing a hat,
While crickets recite jokes on a mat.

Fireflies flutter like tiny lamps,
Dancing around in their funny camps.
Each twinkle's a chuckle, a laugh in the dark,
As night wraps the world in its playful spark.

Supernova Silliness

A star exploded, what funny flare!
It turned into giggles, floating in air.
Planets are spinning, they cannot resist,
Join in the laughter, it's too good to miss.

With comets that whistle as they zoom by,
And asteroids chuckling, oh my, oh my!
Cosmic confetti falls from the sky,
As laughter echoes, oh how it flies!

Cosmic Circus

A ringmaster comet calls all to the show,
While planets juggle in a dazzling glow.
The sun, the spotlight, shines bright and round,
As moons leap through hoops, they spin all around.

Asteroids tumble, like clowns in a spree,
With starry spectators, oh what glee!
Nebulas twist in a spiraled twirl,
In the funhouse of space, every laugh's a pearl.

Jovial Starry Nights

Under the blanket of twinkling bliss,
The stars tell tales with a playful kiss.
Galaxies giggle like small children play,
While stardust sparkles, laughing all day.

Shooting stars race with a cheer and a shout,
Each wishes for laughter, that's what it's about.
The night is a canvas where chuckles are drawn,
In the universe's mirth, we all spawn.

Laughing Light Years

Stars giggle in bright skies,
With tales of wobbly flies.
Planets swirl in dance,
Making comets laugh at chance.

Galaxies spin in joyful jest,
While moons play tag, they're the best.
Light beams tickle the night,
What a silly, starry sight!

Shooting stars wear goofy hats,
While asteroids play peek-a-boo, like cats.
They tumble and tumble, such a sight,
In a universe where joy takes flight.

Stardust tickles our dreams bright,
As laughter echoes in the night.
With every shine, a giggle's shared,
In this space where fun's declared.

Constellation Capers

Orion hides behind the moon,
Whispering jokes, a funny tune.
Cassiopeia struts in flair,
Shooting stars all laugh and stare.

Big Dipper spills his cosmic tea,
As planets jest with glee,
Scorpio dances, tails in twist,
In this stellar, swirling mist.

Pleiades blink and start to giggle,
While comets race and wiggle.
Even black holes can't resist,
In this caper, they insist!

From little meteors to giants grand,
They share laughter across the land.
In the fabric of space, we all partake,
In silly cosmos, joy we make.

Comedic Cosmos

In the vast expanse where puns align,
Planets chuckle, oh so fine.
Nebulas twist in playful glee,
As cosmic clowns join the spree.

A comet cracks a joke so loud,
Even the black holes gather proud.
Asteroids throw a rock 'n' roll,
In the backdrop of the cosmic bowl.

Quasars beam their punchlines bright,
As galaxies giggle through the night.
Light years stretch with every grin,
In the comedy, we all win!

The universe fills with festive cheer,
As laughter vibrates far and near.
In the cosmic play, we find our part,
With a wink and a laugh, it's a cosmic art.

Fickle Footnotes from the Firmament

On starlit pages, jokes unfold,
As comets write the tales bold.
Footnotes dance in the astral haze,
While galaxies giggle in a daze.

Twinkling stars with typo dreams,
Flipping scripts with funny schemes.
Mercury winks with a cheeky grin,
As aliens laugh, let the fun begin!

Eclipses hide behind their masks,
Lost in laughter, forget their tasks.
In this book of space and time,
Every verse is a perfect rhyme.

So pen your wishes beneath the night,
For in each star, there's pure delight.
The firmament quakes with chuckles shared,
In a universe that's truly prepared.

Stellar Smiles

Stars twinkle with glee,
Saturn wears a ring of tea.
The comets laugh as they zoom by,
Dancing through the evening sky.

Jupiter's storms are just a joke,
While asteroids are made of smoke.
The Milky Way beams bright tonight,
With cosmic puns that feel so right.

Planets giggle in their orbits,
While aliens file their reports.
A shooting star wishes to play,
As laughter echoes far away.

So when you gaze at stars above,
Remember space is full of love.
In the universe, fun takes flight,
With every chuckle, pure delight.

Comedic Constellations

The Big Dipper spills its drink,
While Orion gives a wink.
Taurus trips on cosmic dust,
Causing all to laugh, we must.

Little stars play hide and seek,
While comets race at lightning speed.
A puppet show on Mars tonight,
With laughter echoing in flight.

Perseus cracks a silly grin,
As cosmic jokes begin to spin.
Summer's sky, a stage so grand,
Where laughter tumbles through the land.

Constellations share a jest,
Each star a performer at its best.
So when the night is clear and bright,
Join in the fun beneath starlight.

Jovial Journeys Through Space

Rocket ships adorned with cheer,
Zooming past from here to here.
Aliens clown in Moon's cool shade,
As cosmic giggles are relayed.

Saturn's rings, a playful swing,
While Mars invites you out to fling.
Moons dance jigs in playful spree,
Galaxies spin in jubilee.

Asteroids laugh with every crash,
While clever stars make a splash.
A cosmic carnival up high,
Where humor twinkles like the sky.

With every light-year, joy expands,
In playful plots and silly bands.
So float along this frolic space,
Where every smile finds its place.

Giggles in the Galaxy

In nebulae, they toss confetti,
While space whales sing, aren't they petty?
Planets joke around like friends,
With laughter that never ends.

Celestial bodies play charades,
In cosmic courts, they make their grades.
A supernova steals the show,
With bright explosions syncing slow.

Shooting stars take funny bets,
While comets have no regrets.
The universe bursts with delight,
As humor sparkles through the night.

So when you look at skies so grand,
Remember laughter's close at hand.
In every twinkle, every flare,
Are whispers of joy floating in air.

Jovial Journeys Through Space

In a rocket made of candy,
We zoom past stars so dandy.
Galactic giggles fill the air,
Floating marshmallows, we don't care.

Planets dance a silly jig,
While comets spin, a cosmic gig.
Asteroids wink, they're part of the show,
As we sail through the starry glow.

Cosmic clowns with painted smiles,
Playing jokes across the miles.
Shooting stars that tickle your nose,
In this place where laughter glows.

With every laugh, the void's less grim,
Chasing light, we feel the whim.
In this universe of wild delight,
Joy rockets high through the night.

Galaxies in Glee

A star throws a party, bright and bold,
Where planets wear hats of shimmering gold.
Jovial friends with rings that spin,
Take a dip in the laughter within.

Cosmic critters in a playful chase,
Floating freely in this vast space.
Lightyears away, a wink and a grin,
In this dance, we all join in.

Meteor showers rain down fun,
As we slide across the cosmic run.
Each twinkle gleams with a joke concealed,\nA universe of laughter revealed.

Galaxies swirl in a joyous spree,
Echoing laughter in a cosmic sea.
With each spin, the fun expands,
In this realm of giggles and bands.

Moonlit Muses

Underneath a silvery moon,
Crickets chirp a funny tune.
Stars play tricks, make shadows dance,
While the galaxies join in the prance.

Nighttime jesters beam so bright,
Hiding giggles in the starlit night.
A comet slips on cosmic dust,
Blushing deep, it's a must!

Luna laughs at the sun's bright face,
Whispers secrets of space's grace.
Moons of every shape and size,
With goofy grins and laughing eyes.

Here in the dark, joy ignites,
Bouncing beams through starry nights.
Each twinkling wink, a secret told,
In this dance of silver and gold.

The Jovian Jester

Jupiter spins with a playful might,
Wobbling rings in the starry light.
His moons giggle, in a lively swirl,
   Creating chaos as they twirl.

Saturn's youth, with swirling flair,
Throws a party, none can compare.
Asteroids bounce, caught in the fun,
   Under the watch of a cheeky sun.

Neptune sings a haunting tune,
While Uranus chuckles, out of tune.
Galileo grins, his laughter loud,
Crafting joy from the cosmic crowd.

   In the end, the stars unite,
With every burst of pure delight.
The jester's jest lives on through space,
   In a universe of joy and grace.

Starry-Eyed Amusement

In the night, stars twinkle bright,
One whispers, 'Hey, watch me take flight!'
A comet sneezes, sends dust on a spree,
While planets giggle in cosmic glee.

In shadows, the moon plays peek-a-boo,
Clouds lift eyebrows, like they just knew.
Meteor showers, a confetti blast,
As silly old Jupiter spins by fast.

Galaxies swirl in a riddle-filled dance,
While Neptune winks, giving love a chance.
With laughter echoing across the space,
Even black holes can't hide their grace.

Stars trade jokes over drinks made of light,
While Saturn's rings flash like a disco night.
In the vastness where dreams tumble free,
Cosmic laughter is the best, don't you see?

Grins Beyond the Milky Way

Beyond the dust of the Milky sea,
Lies a nebula prankster, filled with glee.
Kosmic kittens chase rays of fun,
While asteroids dance, "Let's run, let's run!"

Planets in orbit with giggles galore,
Taking turns through the vast starry store.
Uranus jokes cause the others to spin,
Laughing out loud as the fun begins.

Wormholes twist with mischievous tricks,
Cars of the cosmos doing quick flicks.
Black hole swirls play peek and hide,
While meteors wave with a zany glide.

Celestial jesters laugh under moons,
Tickled stars sing to their favorite tunes.
Up above, where the chuckles ignite,
Universe smiles in the cover of night.

The Universe's Pranks

In cosmic realms, mischief takes flight,
Where comets wear hats in the shimmering night.
Asteroids roll with a chuckle so loud,
Making quasars laugh, feeling quite proud.

Venus teases Mars, 'You're so red, my friend!'
As jokes echo on, they twist and bend.
Stars fall down, then bounce right back,
A practical jester on the old star track.

Supernovae pop with a surprising roar,
While planets recall jokes from days of yore.
Dancing in rings, laughing like fools,
Galactic giggles break all the rules.

The universe twists in playful delight,
With cosmic jesters igniting the night.
In the grand scheme, nothing quite sinks,
Just playful banter that sparks and winks.

Cosmic Comedy Club

Welcome aboard to the cosmic stage,
Where stars tell stories, wild as a cage.
Galaxies gather, giggling away,
Joining the fun in a humorous sway.

The sun cracks jokes, 'I'm the best in glow!'
While Venus rolls dice, bringing in the show.
'Knock, knock!' cries Mars, 'Who's there?' with flair,
Echoes of laughter spill everywhere.

Asteroids snicker, playing catch-me-if-you-can,
While black holes pull in a reluctant fan.
A supernova says, 'Let's light up the night!'
Creating a comedy, pure delight.

In this comedy club, laughter's a must,
Even the silence is filled with trust.
The universe spins with joy and surprise,
As joy rides the waves, reaching the skies.

The Humor of Nebulas

In a cloud of cotton candy bright,
Stars giggle, twinkling with delight.
Galaxies swirl in a playful dance,
Making black holes pause and prance.

Planets jest with rings of glee,
While comets wink as they fly free.
Asteroids laugh as they bounce and roll,
"Catch us if you can!" is the goal.

Meteor showers fall like jokes,
Chasing the cosmos as laughter pokes.
Even supernovae burst in mirth,
Exploding with joy, spreading their worth.

So look to the sky, if you feel low,
The universe chuckles; let the fun flow!
In every twinkle and cosmic glitch,
Find humor hidden, scratch that itch.

Witty Whispers from the Cosmos

Milky Way spills secrets at night,
Star clusters giggle, oh what a sight!
They tease the moon, with its silver glow,
"Don't get too big; we all know you're slow."

Galactic winds carry puns afar,
As shooting stars dash like a quirky car.
"Did you hear the one about space-time?"
Even the comets find it sublime!

Radio waves crack jokes in the dark,
While quasars brighten with a cosmic spark.
"Why did the black hole refuse to play?
It couldn't let go, not even for a day!"

So tune into laughter through cosmic beams,
The universe whispers, igniting our dreams.
In the vastness, find joy in the jest,
For every giggle, the stars are blessed.

Playful Pulsars

Tick-tock go the light beams bright,
Pulsars play peek-a-boo, what a sight!
With each spin, they burst into cheer,
Sending messages for those who hear.

"Why did the neutron star get a ride?"
"Too dense to walk, it couldn't decide!"
Silly magnets hold them tight,
Laughing in rhythm, what pure delight!

They count the seconds with witty flair,
In the orbit of laughter, they're always there.
"Two black holes walk into a bar,
The bartender says, 'You two are bizarre!'"

So dance with the beats of starlit tunes,
In the arms of the universe, under the moons.
A symphony of chuckles, a joyous embrace,
In this cosmic ballet, we all find our place.

Joyful Orbits

Saturn spins with a ringed smile,
Jupiter winks from a cosmic mile.
Earth chuckles as it spins on a dime,
"Hey everyone, perfect space-time!"

Venus flirts with a glimmering grace,
While Mars brags about its rough race.
"Did you hear the joke about space debris?
It's just garbage, but oh so free!"

With every rotation, laughter takes flight,
Trailing through galaxies, spreading delight.
Each planet swings in this grand cosmic ball,
And the stars above giggle, they're having a ball!

So join in the fun, let your heart soar,
With each orbital twist, there's so much in store.
In this joyous ping-pong of heavenly cheer,
The universe whispers, "Laughter is near!"

Galactic Glee

Stars wink above, a laughing sight,
Planets spin, a jolly flight.
Galaxies giggle, bright and bold,
As comets tell tales, ages old.

Asteroids dance, a cosmic jig,
Orbiting moons, they twist and wig.
Nebulas burst with colors, whoopee,
In this vast space, joy's the key!

Black holes grin, with a cheeky pull,
While quasar beams make jokes that rule.
Space dust tickles the Milky Way,
In this universe, we laugh and play.

So join the fun, in starlit cheer,
In the sky's grand show, there's nothing to fear!
For laughter shines, the brightest star,
In galaxies far, in dreams we are.

Cosmic Comedy Chronicles

In the vastness where the funny flies,
Meteor showers drop jokes from the skies.
Astro beings crack cosmic puns,
With laughter echoing, we've just begun.

Planets in line, they jest and poke,
The sun can't help but burst with a joke.
Saturn's rings spin with gleeful chimes,
While starlit giggles dance through the times.

Each universe spins, a tale to share,
Of supernovae that shoot through the air.
Rusty robots share tales of their wrecks,
While all-stars play just for fun, what the heck!

Galactic antics in celestial dance,
Space jesters make the cosmos prance.
In this funny orbit, we unite,
Finding joy in stars, under moonlight.

Universes of Humor

From distant worlds where laughter thrives,
Planets chuckle, and humor arrives.
Aliens giggle with tales of delight,
Under starlit skies, we share the night.

Nebulas shimmer with playful jest,
While quarks and leptons take a rest.
Cosmic pranks in the stardust roam,
In the vast expanse, we find our home.

Elliptical galaxies with smiles so bright,
Wormholes giggle, a comical sight.
Gravity pulls but can't weigh down fun,
In these infinite realms, laughter's begun.

So gather round in this universe wide,
With starlight jokes, humor our guide.
For in every corner, with just a spark,
The universe laughs, lighting up the dark.

Nebula's Nonsense

In the clouds where stardust dreams,
Galaxies giggle in silver beams.
A comet slips on its cosmic tail,
Laughing hard, it starts to sail.

Planets play hide and seek at night,
Jupiter winks with all its might.
Saturn spins rings in a silly dance,
While Mars pranks Venus with a glance.

Stars swap names for a wild jest,
Orion's belt plays dress-up in jest.
The Moon steals cheese from a passing ship,
As meteors chuckle on their trip.

Cosmic beings in a joyful spree,
Creating laughter, wild and free.
In the vastness, humor flows,
Where the universe's laughter glows.

Celestial Pranks of the Stars

Twinkling lights with mischief share,
Playing tricks from here to there.
A shooting star calls out your name,
But in its wake, it's all a game.

Galaxies swirl in playful spins,
While comets giggle with their fins.
Asteroids rock to a quirky tune,
Bouncing happily around the moon.

The Sun hides behind fluffy clouds,
Peeking out amidst cosmic crowds.
It tells a joke, and planets roar,
While starlight dances upon the floor.

With laughter echoing through the void,
Cosmic jokes never feel annoyed.
In the night, where wonders soar,
The universe laughs forevermore.

Solar System Shenanigans

In a whirl of cosmic cheer,
Planets giggle, drawing near.
Earth plays tricks on the Moon's glow,
While Venus dances with a flow.

Neptune's blues and Mars's red,
Joke with light that they spread.
Mercury zips, a speedy tease,
While Saturn twirls in the solar breeze.

Asteroids toss some comic pies,
While shooting stars paint the skies.
Galaxies trade their bright reflections,
In stellar pranks, they find connections.

Laughter echoes through the dark,
As every comet leaves its mark.
In the silence of the cosmic night,
Joy ignites the endless light.

Milky Way Mischief

In the spiral arms of the Milky Way,
Stars tell stories of a funny play.
A black hole yawns in a great big grin,
As light gets lost in a cosmic spin.

Nebulas giggle with colorful flair,
While space dust tickles the solar air.
The universe whispers jokes divine,
As the galaxies twist and intertwine.

Supernovae burst with a pop and clap,
While planets fall into a cosmic nap.
Comets chase light with a playful streak,
Creating laughter at the universe's peak.

In this dance of starry delight,
Every gaze brings joy through the night.
And as we ponder the vast embrace,
Mischief blooms in every place.

Comets with a Sense of Humor

A comet dashed through the night,
With a wink and a tail full of light.
It danced past the stars with a jig,
Leaving planets to laugh at its gig.

Asteroids chuckled as they rolled,
Telling jokes in the cosmic cold.
They bounced off each other in glee,
"Did you hear the one about a flea?"

Galaxies spun in a wild embrace,
Twinkling bright in the vast, open space.
With every whirl, there's a wink on display,
"Watch out for the prankster on Milky Way!"

So when you gaze to the sky at night,
Remember the laughter that takes flight.
For in the heavens, fun's on the rise,
With comets and stars wearing laughable guise.

The Lightness of Being in Space

Floating high with a smile so wide,
An astronaut giggles, taking the ride.
With zero G, the jokes can soar,
As moons spin tales of the cosmic floor.

Shooting stars flicker, make wishes fly,
"Why can't an asteroid ever tell a lie?"
They bask in the glow of the Milky Way,
Cracking up as they float and sway.

In the vastness, a neutrino beams,
With laughter that echoes through space's dreams.
Gravity fails, but humor is sound,
In this lightness, pure joy is found.

So when you look up at the endless dark,
Know that in laughter, there's always a spark.
For up in the void, the jesters sing,
A funny cosmos, where giggles take wing.

Celestial Jests

In a galaxy far, one star had a prance,
Wobbling about in a comedic dance.
It juggled small planets with glee,
While the comets clapped, "What a sight to see!"

The moons joined in with a twirl and a spin,
"Oh, let us join, let the laughter begin!"
They swung through the rings with a cheer so bright,
Spreading joy in the deep, starry night.

The black holes, mysterious yet sly,
Whispered jokes that made stardust cry.
"Knock, knock," they'd say, "Who's there?" with a grin,
"A little more matter - come dance, my kin!"

So toss your gaze to the shimmering sphere,
Feel the humor that's floating near.
For in the universe, the jesters play,
Crafting laughter that lights up the way.

A Symphony of Space Laughter

In the cosmos, laughter plays a tune,
As planets hum under the light of the moon.
Stars twinkle slyly, sharing a jest,
While meteors race, never taking a rest.

Nebulas giggle, swirling in hues,
Making punchlines with cosmic views.
"With a wink from the sun, bright and bold,
Who knew the universe was so uncontrolled?"

A comet passed by with a cheeky wave,
"Is space just a vacuum, or is it a rave?"
The echoes of humor bounced off the seams,
Creating a symphony of cosmic dreams.

So when you look at the night sky's frame,
Remember the laughter, the joy, the game.
For in this grand ballet of stars up above,
Lies a universe playful, a testament of love.

Whispers of the Galaxies

Stars giggle in the night,
Planets spin with delight.
Nebulas swirl in a whirl,
While comets wink and twirl.

The moons share silly tales,
Of space bears and their gales.
Shooting stars, they jump and play,
In the vastness, they sway.

Galactic beings chuckle loud,
Befriending each starry cloud.
Laughter echoes through the void,
In this cosmos, joy's alloyed.

The cosmos hums a bright tune,
Underneath the silver moon.
As worlds dance in joyous cheer,
A universal laugh we hear.

Moonbeam Mirth

Moonbeams peek through the trees,
Caressing faces with ease.
They tickle the quiet night,
Bringing giggles, pure delight.

Crickets chirp in sweet refrain,
Their rhythms cause laughter's gain.
Even owls hoot with a grin,
Join the fun, let the night begin!

Stars spin tales of silly dreams,
Where nothing's ever what it seems.
The night sky plays its own prank,
Filling hearts with joy in rank.

Beneath the cosmic spread,
Laughter dances, joy widespread.
Each playful glimmer, a spark,
Lighting up the playful dark.

Jupiter's Jovial Jests

Jupiter laughs with thunderous glee,
Its storms are amusing, come see!
With clouds that poke fun at the sun,
In this playground, they all run.

Its moons play tag 'round its belt,
In a radiant game, they've knelt.
Twisting and twirling, oh so spry,
Creating chuckles that reach the sky.

Comedians of the astral scene,
In this circus, joy's routine.
Gravity's pull adds to the fun,
As the gas giant shines like a pun.

From swirling storms to jovial jest,
This giant knows how to impress.
In the dance of planets, so divine,
Laughter echoes, a cosmic line.

Comet's Comedic Dance

A comet zooms with a bright tail,
Comically swift, it will not fail.
It streaks through space with cheeky grace,
Leaving laughter in its trace.

Whirling past with a whoosh and a wink,
Its presence makes stardust think.
Round and round, it twirls and spins,
Releasing joy—the laughter begins!

Asteroids watch with open eyes,
As the comet performs in the skies.
Each swoop and dive causes a laugh,
A cosmic joke on life's big path.

In its wake, silliness flows,
Echoing through the cosmic throes.
From afar, all planets rejoice,
Hailed by the comets' jovial voice.

Chortles in the Cosmic Sea

In the vastness where comets dart,
Galaxies giggle, each playing their part.
Stars throw jokes like a playful net,
While black holes belly-laugh with no regret.

Planets spin in a synchronized dance,
Winking at each other, a merry chance.
Asteroids chuckle, tumbling with glee,
In the cosmic playground where all are free.

Nebulae shimmer with colors so bright,
Mysterious riddles that tickle the night.
Pulsars pulsate with a rhythmic jest,
As laughter erupts from the universe's chest.

So let's float among these radiant souls,
Sharing the joy that tickles and rolls.
In this endless expanse, we find our delight,
A whimsical voyage through the starry night.

The Universe Winks

Planets with smiles, oh what a sight,
Winking at each other in the quiet night.
Stardust sprinkled with laughter and cheer,
Whispers of giggles from galaxies near.

Astrological jokes rise like the sun,
With every constellation, the fun's never done.
A cosmic punchline that echoes through space,
Each twinkling star wearing a grin on its face.

Meteor showers, a sky full of gags,
Leaving behind their sparkling flags.
Shooting stars laugh as they zip on by,
Promising wishes as they wave goodbye.

So keep looking up, in the night so vast,
For luminous jesters, their shadows will cast.
In the embrace of the infinite play,
The universe winks, come join in the fray.

Light-Hearted Luminaries

Beaming bright lights with playful grins,
Laughter cascades as the night begins.
Stars share tickles in radiant hues,
While lunar beams scatter joyful news.

These vibrant orbs, with their radiant tunes,
Dance in circles, like silly buffoons.
A comet swoops by with a glittery jest,
Leaving behind a luminous quest.

Solar flares crackle, a fiery tease,
While Saturn's rings twirl with such ease.
Every supernova bursts with delight,
Expanding the joy in the tapestry of night.

So let us bask in this luminous glow,
Where each twinkle makes the laughter flow.
In the adorable play of the cosmic light,
The universe celebrates, oh what a sight!

Constellation Cackles

Orion's belt jingles with mirthful tones,
While Ursa Major shares giggling groans.
Aqua stars chortle as they take their place,
In the comedy show of the infinite space.

Little dippers splash in a playful spree,
With each gag, they set the cosmos free.
A quasar winks from its dazzling perch,
Provoking the void to join in the search.

Galaxies swirl in a whimsical dance,
Spinning tales that put us in a trance.
Joyful nebulae puff out their cheeks,
As laughter bursts out, in cosmic peaks.

Count the stars, one jovial jest,
In the tapestry woven, laughter's the best.
From the twinkling skies, let chuckles beam,
In this stellar realm, we all can dream.

Giggles from the Great Beyond

The moon wore a hat, quite absurd,
As stars snickered softly, unheard.
A comet quipped, with a wink so sly,
'Why do we twinkle? Just to reply!'

The planets pranced in a jovial dance,
While asteroids tumbled, taking a chance.
'We're rocks, but we're funny!' they joyfully shouted,
As cosmic laughter filled the space, unclouded.

Eclipses chuckled, tickling the skies,
While galaxies giggled, all in disguise.
For in the vastness where shadows play,
Laughter is found in a brilliant ballet.

So when you look up, remember this night,
The universe laughs, it's a delightful sight.
With chuckles and cheers, it spins without end,
In the great unknown, where humor transcends.

Laughing Comets

Comets zoom by with grins so wide,
Trailing laughter, they joyfully glide.
'Catch us if you can!' they gleefully tease,
As planets spin round, proclaiming their fees.

In a cosmic race, the stars take a turn,
With sparkles of joy, and laughter to burn.
They play hide and seek in the Milky Way's glow,
Chasing starlight, putting on quite a show.

Supernovae burst with bright, boisterous cheer,
'Look at us go!' they proclaim from near.
Galactic giggles echo across the night,
In a universe painted with whimsical light.

So join in their frolic, let laughter take flight,
In the vast cosmic sea, we're all shining bright.
Watch the comets dance, and join in the fun,
In the sport of the stars, we're all number one!

Whimsical Wakefulness

In the still of the night, the stars share a grin,
Whispers of mirth on a playful whim.
Each twinkle a joke, each blink a delight,
In this whimsical wakefulness, all comes to light.

The constellations giggle, winking with glee,
While meteors dash, daring to be free.
'Wish upon us!' they sing with delight,
'For we bring smiles to the darkest of nights.'

Gravity chuckles, pulling us near,
In this dance of the cosmos, we have nothing to fear.
With a jiggle of laughter, the heavens unfold,
Stories of whimsy, a joy to behold.

So dream under skies that shimmer and glow,
Remember the laughter in all that you know.
For no matter how silent the night may appear,
The universe whispers, 'Let laughter draw near.'

A Satirical Solar System

In this solar realm, planets act quirky,
Mercury's swift, but oftentimes jerky.
Venus rolls eyes, with a smirk and a pout,
'Things get hot here, that's without a doubt!'

Mars boasts his red, 'I'm the warrior bold!'
While Jupiter chuckles, 'You're just over-sold.'
The rings of Saturn, like a joke on a stage,
Spin in laughter; oh, what a page!

Uranus giggles, hiding behind gas,
While Neptune swirls, in a cool, misty class.
Pluto peeks in, 'Am I still in the game?'
'Of course!' said the stars; 'It's all just a name!'

With cosmic banter and a sparkly wink,
Each planet a jester, makes us stop and think.
In the satire of space, we find our way,
In the laughter of worlds, come out and play!

Galaxy's Grinning Gaze

In the cosmos, stars collide,
With laughter dancing, they abide.
Nebulas twirl in silken glee,
As planets waltz in jubilee.

Shooting stars with silly streaks,
Tickle moons and make them speak.
Black holes hum a quirky tune,
While comets bounce like a balloon.

Astrological Antics

Zodiac signs play hide and seek,
In carefree skies, they're strong and sleek.
Capricorns jump with joyful grace,
While Leos strut in outer space.

Virgos juggle cosmic dust,
And Libras spin with merry thrust.
Every sign, a quirky show,
Underneath the stellar glow.

Starry-Skied Shenanigans

The Milky Way hosts a grand parade,
With twinkling stars unafraid.
Saturn wears a silly hat,
While Venus dances with the cat.

Galaxies giggle as they sway,
In the ballet of the night and day.
Constellations trade their pranks,
While asteroids perform in ranks.

Orion's Quirky Quips

Orion winks with a sly grin,
His belt jingles, let the fun begin!
Sirius snickers, a bright-eyed glare,
While stars perform without a care.

Laughter echoes through the space,
In this waltz of light and grace.
Each twinkle tells a playful tale,
As galaxies rise, senses sail.

Celestial Whimsy

The stars play pranks in midnight's hue,
Dancing in circles, just for you.
Planets spin tales of silly dreams,
While moons whisper secrets, or so it seems.

A comet's tail tickles the sleepy sun,
As space critters giggle, having their fun.
Asteroids juggling in a cosmic show,
With laughter echoing, high and low.

Nebulas chuckle, bright colors collide,
As starlight bounces in a joyful ride.
Galaxies spiral, a festive parade,
With every twinkle, a grand charade.

In the cosmic playground, jesters fly,
With light-years tickling the vast night sky.
So here's to the cosmos, wild and bright,
Where every laugh sparks a starry light.

Stardust Smirks

Twinkling eyes in the wide expanse,
Stars clap their hands, inviting a dance.
A little black hole with a cheeky grin,
Swallows up laughter, let the joy begin.

Meteor showers like confetti rain,
Splashing in space, impervious to pain.
Galactic jesters, with each leap and bound,
Create a ruckus, a joyful sound.

Winking at planets that roll and glide,
Comets tease with their bright tails wide.
In the quiet void, whispers of cheer,
Echo through ether, for all to hear.

Celestial beings with a penchant for fun,
Chasing dark shadows, on the run.
The universe giggles, a grand old time,
In the cosmic circus, so sublime!

Galactic Grins and Giggles

A supernova bursts in a flurry of lights,
As galaxies tumble, reaching new heights.
Stars snicker loudly, each shimmer a joke,
While stardust clouds puff like a puff of smoke.

Planets spin tales with goofy delight,
Rings giggle softly in the velvet night.
Cosmic balloons bobbing, laughter in tow,
Creating a show that's their own to bestow.

Space dust bounces like playful sprites,
While bright quasars tease the lonely nights.
Every pulsar shines with a wink and a nod,
The universe winks, it's jovially odd.

Jupiter's storm sings a rollicking tune,
As Saturn's gaps hum under the moon.
In this vast playground, let joy interlace,
With cosmic giggles, our hearts embrace.

Comet's Quirky Quarreling

A comet veers off, both cheeky and spry,
Tickles Orion, who lets out a sigh.
In a spin of laughter, they tumble and play,
Arguments sparkle in a whimsical way.

Mars joins the brawl, with a face full of red,
While Venus chuckles, "You've lost your thread!"
Galactic disputes over snacks from the sun,
Each star is a judge, to see who has fun.

Asteroids cheer as the chaos ensues,
With constellations forming comical views.
In cosmic bickering, there's joy to unfold,
As starlight twinkles the stories retold.

So here in the heavens, let laughter soar high,
Though objects collide, they know how to fly.
In a playful squabble, their spirits unite,
In the vast universe, where love shines bright.

Radiant Revelry

In the night sky, stars whisper light,
With giggles that twinkle, oh what a sight!
The moon winks softly, grinning so wide,
As comets play tag on a cosmic ride.

Galaxies swirl in a waltz so grand,
While asteroids dance, they don't quite land.
With laughter that echoes, from afar they beam,
Creating a cosmic, celestial dream.

Shooting stars make wishes, but who can tell,
If wishes come true or just chuckle and dwell?
With vibrant colors splashed through the sky,
Even dark matter can't help but sigh.

So let's toast to the orbs that laugh and glow,
For space is a stage with a marvelous show.
As planets all giggle and share their delight,
We'll dance in their shadows, beneath the moonlight.

Stars in Stitches

The night unfolds with a glimmering grin,
As starlight bubbles, it tickles within.
Nebulas giggle, splattering hues,
While black holes burp with a mighty, rich muse.

Planets spin tales of their zany old days,
Of joyful collisions and playful displays.
While space dust flutters like laughter in air,
Creating a tapestry without a care.

Meteor showers play catch with the dusk,
As cosmic confetti turns dark skies to husk.
Each burst of delight lights up the vast dome,
While laughter in space feels surprisingly home.

So when you gaze up, just know they're all there,
With chuckles and giggles to share everywhere.
In the vastness above, with joy intertwined,
A universe bursting with humor, unconfined.

Quasar Quips

A quasar giggles, with lightyears of jest,
Sending forth messages of cosmic zest.
With jokes in the ether, they shimmer and sway,
Lighting up dark voids in a marvelous way.

Wormholes whisper secrets that make planets chuckle,
While supernovas burst in a sparkling shuffle.
Each twist of time is a punchline anew,
Spinning tales of the cosmos for me and for you.

The cosmos is vast, but fun's not scarce,
With black holes that wink and show flair in their dance.
Even starlight giggles as it travels afar,
A tapestry woven from each shining star.

So gaze at the heavens and join in the cheer,
For laughter's a language all beings hold dear.
In the play of the spheres, let joy take its course,
As every bright quasar brings forth a new force.

The Playful Paradox of Planets

In the realm of the skies, planets romp and play,
With gravity jokes that just float away.
Mars teases Venus, saying, 'Look at me shine!'
While Jupiter's storms whirl in a dance so fine.

Earth laughs at the chaos, spins in delight,
As moons pull and tug, creating a sight.
Even Saturn with rings can't help but boast,
'Got the best bling, now let's raise a toast!'

Asteroids plot mischief in their rocky ballet,
While cosmic winds carry their giggles astray.
Each rotation spins tales that make us all grin,
As universe's jesters, the fun never thins.

So watch the sky's show, let your heart feel light,
For the planets are laughing, dancing through night.
In this playful paradox, let joyful hearts meet,
As the universe chuckles at its own funny beat.

Jovial Stars Align

The moon wore pajamas, quite bright and round,
Juggling comets in the cosmic playground.
Stars giggle and twinkle, a gleeful parade,
As planets do cartwheels, unafraid of the shade.

A sunbeam tickles a cheeky old sprite,
Who dances on meteorites, oh what a sight!
Galaxies spin, laughing at fate,
While orbits are tangled, it's all first-rate!

The nebulae chuckle, paint colors so wild,
Each spiral like laughter that's joyfully styled.
In this grand universe, so messy and bright,
Even black holes grin—what a galactic delight!

So raise up your glasses to the night sky's fun,
For laughter's the light, and we're all on the run.
With humor as vast as the starlit expanse,
Let's giggle and sparkle—join in the dance!

Chortles in the Asteroids

Asteroids tumble with a raucous cheer,
Making jokes as they bounce, oh my dear!
A rock with a grin sings a silly old song,
While others play tag, all the day long.

Comets pass by with a whoosh and a twirl,
Showing off tails that whirl like a girl.
In the cosmic bazaar of laughter and play,
The universe joins in—hip hip hooray!

A funny old satellite spins in delight,
Telling tales of the planets that danced in the night.
"Oh, can't you just see?" giggles a wily old star,
"I tripped on a quasar, and here we are!"

So let's toast to the rocks and the giggles they make,
In the orbit of joy, let's celebrate and quake.
For humor's the glue in this galaxy's glue,
Bring out the laughter—there's plenty for you!

Celestial Antics

A puff of stardust tickled the sun,
Causing it to giggle—oh what fun!
Planets all wobbled on their merry-go-round,
While asteroids chuckled with a lighthearted sound.

The rings of Saturn jangled like bells,
As Icarus giggled from his fiery spells.
Jupiter rumbled with laughter so deep,
While Neptune sulked but swallowed a peep.

A meteor dashed by with a wink and a grin,
Yelling, "Catch me if you can—let the games begin!"
The cosmos erupting in a jovial spree,
Tickles and giggles—come laugh here with me!

So join in the fun of this cosmic charade,
For laughter's the starlight that will never fade.
In the great vast expanse, humor's the key,
So come, my stargazers, and frolic with me!

A Cosmic Carousel of Laughs

Round and round on the cosmic ride,
Stars burst into laughter, and they won't hide.
Galaxies whirl, in a dizzying spin,
While comets play tag, let the giggles begin!

The Milky Way's a fairground of fun,
Where laughter is universal, for everyone.
Neon bright flares shoot across the void,
Chortles from quasars cannot be destroyed!

Each twinkling light like a smile in the night,
As black holes bumblingly try to take flight.
A meta-merry-go, spun with delight,
Dancing celestial beings gleeful and bright.

When stardust falls gently, it tickles the toes,
We laugh and we spin as the cosmos glows.
So come, be a part of this hilarity grand,
In a joyful loop, hand in hand, we stand!

Laughter Among the Stars

In the sky, a twinkling tease,
Stars tell jokes on cosmic breeze.
Planets roll with glee tonight,
Shooting stars in pure delight.

Galaxies spin in playful jest,
Laughing loud, they are the best.
Comets swoosh like clowns in flight,
Glowing orbs in joyous light.

Meteorites with silly faces,
Dance around in starry races.
Black holes chuckle, swirling fast,
While light-years fly by in a blast.

Saturn's rings, a playful jest,
Joke with moons around their nest.
In this vast, fun-filled expanse,
The universe invites to dance.

Cosmic Giggles at Midnight

Beneath the blanket of the night,
Stars exchange their playful light.
Nebulae, in colors bright,
Guffaw at the moon's delight.

Aliens in spacesuits grin,
Telling tales of where they've been.
Asteroids bounce with joyful cheer,
Whispering secrets for all to hear.

Satellites wink with knowing smiles,
Orbiting tales for endless miles.
Galactic puns that twist and twirl,
In this universal swirl.

Wormholes giggle, pulling near,
Time and space, a funny sphere.
Even black holes join the fun,
Sucking laughter, one by one.

When Planets Play

Planets gather in a line,
Playing games, they intertwine.
Venus winks, while Mars is bold,
Jupiter laughs, a sight to behold.

In gravity's grasp, they spin around,
Making music, a cosmic sound.
Saturn's rings slid with a swirl,
It's a merry star-studded whirl!

Neptune sneezes, and laughs break free,
Releasing giggles across the sea.
While Mercury zips, quick as a flash,
Making comments in a comical dash.

In this solar playground so wide,
Life's a joke, there's no need to hide.
Together they play, both near and far,
With chirpy laughter from each shining star.

Moonlight Mirth

In the stillness of the moon's bright gaze,
Nighttime jesters begin their phase.
Moonbeams slide in silver shoes,
Telling tales of whimsical views.

Crickets chirp with laughter's beat,
While owls hoot in their retreat.
Silhouettes of trees in playful sway,
Joining in this merry ballet.

Stars flicker like a caravan,
They chuckle loud, oh what a plan!
Even clouds join in the jest,
Drifting by, a fluffy guest.

With every twinkle, every sound,
Joy upon the night is found.
In moonlit laughter's gleeful might,
We find our smiles in pure delight.

www.ingramcontent.com/pod-product-compliance
Lightning Source LLC
Chambersburg PA
CBHW051654160426
43209CB00004B/894